"All the darkness in the world cannot extinguish the light of a single candle."
Francis of Assisi

List of Works:

- Giotto di Bondone: The Stigma of St. Francis, altar panel, detail: The bird preaching, Paris, France (Cover)
- Coppo di Marcovaldo: Saint Francis with scenes from his life, around 1240, Florence, Basilica Santa Croce, Florence, Italy (pp. 2-3)
- Cristoforo Cortese, 1399-1445: Francis in glory, detail: book painting, Musée Marmottan, Paris, France (pp. 5 and 32)
- Giotto di Bondone: 28 scenes from the Life of Francis, frescoes, c. 1330, Basilica of San Francesco, Assisi, Italy: The Allegory of Poverty, p. 9: The Dream of Pope Innocent III (detail), p. 11: Saint Francis gives his cloak, p. 14: Homily before Pope Honorius III. (details), p. 17: The bird preaching, p. 21: Expulsion of the devils from Arezzo, pp. 24 and 26: The Christmas celebration in the forest of Greccio (details), pp. 24-25.
- Sassetta (Stefano di Giovanni di Consolo da Cartona): The Tapestry of St. Francis, de Borgo San Sepolcro, c. 1437-44, National Gallery, London, Great Britain (p. 13)
- Fra Angelico: Fire testimony of St. Francis before the Sultan, 1429, Lindenau Museum, Altenburg, Germany (p. 15)
- Taddeo di Bartolo: The spring miracle of St. Francis, fragment of a Predella, 1403, Landesmuseum Hannover, Germany (p. 19)
- Jan van Eyck: stigmatization of St. Francis, detail, 1432, Galleria Sabauda, Turin, Italy (p.20)
- Domenico Ghirlandaio: Histories of St. Francis, The Resurrection of the Boy, 1485, Sasseti Chapel, Santa Trinita, Florence, Italy (pp.22-23)
- Martin Schongauer: The Birth of Christ, the main altar of the Dominicans, c. 1470, Unterlinden Museum, Colmar, France (p. 25)
- Sassetta (Stefano di Giovanni di Consolo da Cartona): The wolf of Gubbio, the tapestry of St. Francis, De Borgo San Sepolcro, c. 1437-44, National Gallery, London, Great Britain (p. 27)
- Taddeo di Bartolo: Francis preaching to the birds, 1403, Landesmuseum Hannover, Germany (p. 28)
- Giovanni Bellini: St. Francis in the Desert, 1480, The Frick Collection, New York, United States (p. 29)
- Master of St. Francis: the preaching of Francis, around 1255-1260, San Francesco, Assisi, Italy (pp. 30-31)

minedition

English edition published 2017 by Michael Neugebauer Publishing Ltd., Hong Kong

Text and concept copyright © 2014 Géraldine Elschner
Image data: © Bridgeman, Paris, for all pictures except pages 19 and 28
© Artothek, Weilheim, Germany, for pages 19 and 28
Rights arranged with "minedition" Rights and Licensing AG, Zurich, Switzerland.

Michael Neugebauer Publishing Ltd.,
Unit 28, 5/F, Metro Centre, Phase 2,No.21 Lam Hing Street, Kowloon Bay, Kowloon, Hong Kong
Phone +852 2807 1711, e-mail: info@minedition.com
This edition was printed in May 2017 at L.Rex Printing Co Ltd.
3/F., Blue Box Factory Building, 25 Hing Wo Street, Tin Wan, Aberdeen, Hong Kong, China
Typesetting in Silentium Pro Roman I
Library of Congress Cataloging-in-Publication Data available upon request.

ISBN 978-988-8341-44-3
10 9 8 7 6 5 4 3 2 1
First Impression

For more information please visit our website: www.minedition.com

FRANCIS OF ASSISI
HE WHO SPOKE WITH ANIMALS

Selected and told by Géraldine Elschner
With quotations from Pope Francis

minedition

Who is the man with the hood who walks barefoot? He does not wear elegant clothes, no coat embroidered with gold threads.

No wonder, for his bride in this picture is not a fine lady of the world but poverty itself. Francis sought poverty as his companion in life.

He was born into one of the richest families in Assisi.

Ŝ PAUPTAS

As a youth, he liked to listen to the music of the troubadours. He danced. He often celebrated with friends. After a war with a neighboring town, he spent a year in prison. Then he became ill.

Now he had time to think...
only fun and pleasure: surely that was not his purpose in life?

While praying in the ruins of the church of San Damiano, he heard a voice, a call that seemed to come from the crucifix. "Francis, go and rebuild My house."

Save the House of God? He, Francis?

Francis sold precious bolts of cloth and even his horse to rebuild the ruined church. He also helped rebuild other churches in the area.

One day he even gave a poor knight his coat.

"Do you not have anything better to do?" exclaimed his father. The rich cloth merchant was furious with his ungrateful son for squandering away his hard-earned money and wasting time with beggars!

In fact, Francis did have better things to do. His decision had been made.

"Money shall serve, not reign!"

Pope Francis • Address to the new ambassadors accredited to the Holy See from Kyrgyzstan, Antigua and Barbuda, Luxembourg and Botswana, May 16, 2013

To be close to the poor and closer to God, he had to abandon everything.

"I renounce my heritage," he said. On the square of Assisi, he took off his clothes and laid them at the feet of his stunned father. A purple cloak, fine shoes, costly clasps: he no longer wanted all that wealth. A coarse-woven robe, with a cord for a belt, would be enough for him. From then on, only his Father in Heaven would accompany him.

No sooner had he said farewell to his father than he met a leper on the street. Francis started to run away, but once again, the voice called. Francis returned to embrace the outcast. A new happiness filled his heart. He knew now where his path would lead him.

> *"In this world of globalization,*
> *we have fallen into the globalization*
> *of indifference."*
>
> Pope Francis • Sermon on Lampedusa, July 8, 2013

Far away from the splendid world, Francis, together with a few brothers, founded the Franciscan Order, named after him. With a happy heart, he traveled from town to town, preaching. His words found their way directly into people's hearts. He spoke with such power and warmth that everyone listened to his message of peace— simple men, a pope, a sultan.

"What does it mean to cultivate
and protect the earth..."

Pope Francis • General Audience, St. Peter's Square, Rome, June 5, 2013

Even the birds flew to him in droves.

Who listened to whom?

When they sang, he was still and admired the beauty of their song. When he began preaching, the swallows were silent.

For the turtle doves, he built a nest.

For the earthworm, he gave protection.

Francis believed, whether large or small, they were all God's creations, and each deserved respect.

> *"...Let the world grow responsibly, transform it into a garden, into a habitable place for all."*
>
> Pope Francis • General Audience, St. Peter's Square, Rome, June 5, 2013

As often as he could, Francis returned to nature, which he particularly loved. It was there that he was the closest to the Creator - in the meadows full of flowers, among the trees, and with the animals. One day when he went to the mountains, a peasant lent him his donkey. The man was thirsty, and so Francis prayed, and soon water began to flow between the stones.

Everyone had a place in the beautiful Canticle of the Sun, which he composed to express his brotherhood with creation:

"Sister Water," useful and precious, "Brother Wind," "Brother Fire," powerful and strong, and "Mother Earth" who feeds us.

·S·francisc·

While he prayed, lonely in the mountains, an angel appeared in the sky, as if nailed to a cross. The five wounds of Christ were given to him and remained on Francis's hands, his feet, and on his side. He now resembled Jesus even more.

Miracles happen.

In Arezzo, torn and troubled by civil war, Francis sent his follower Sylvester to the city gate. "Go and drive out all evil spirits!"

He did so, and immediately peace and quiet returned to the city.

When a child died, Francis appeared and brought the boy back to life.

The joy was great!

And how great the thanks and the honor for this extraordinary man of God.

He, who was so small as a man, but so great in soul and heart, was certainly holy.

One Christmas in the city of Greccio Francis prepared to hold an evening service. He sent an ox and a donkey to a cave. He filled the manger with fresh hay. There lay the child.

The poverty of the new-born king: he was to speak of it tonight. He wanted to show it so that everyone could feel what happened in Bethlehem on that holy night.

It was the first nativity scene, as we know it today...

"The culture of the encounter, the culture of dialogue: this is the only way to peace."

Pope Francis • Angelus, Petersplatz, Rome, September 1, 2013

Whether gentle or wild, no one remained unmoved when his hand reached out.

It was the same with the wolf of Gubbio, who had frightened the whole area.

"Brother Wolf," said Francis confidently, drawing a cross over his head. He persuaded the persecuted animal not to attack anyone. He also made the inhabitants of the city promise not to let the wolf starve and to care for him. The enemy is only the one who no longer finds his place between heaven and earth.

From then on, so it was told, the wolf went peacefully from door to door, and no dog barked at him.

Ill, and almost blind, the "Troubadour of God" hardly left his refuge in nature. There, near Assisi, where he was born, "our brother, death," as Francis himself called him, came and took him.

Today, he remains the man of poverty and peace, the man full of love and respect for creation, who cared for the little ones and protected everyone. The man who spoke to the animals.

October 4 was named World Animal Protection Day in his honor.

For his closeness to nature, Saint Francis was also named the patron saint of environmental protection and ecology by Pope John Paul II in 1979.

Now as then, Francis shares a closeness to all.

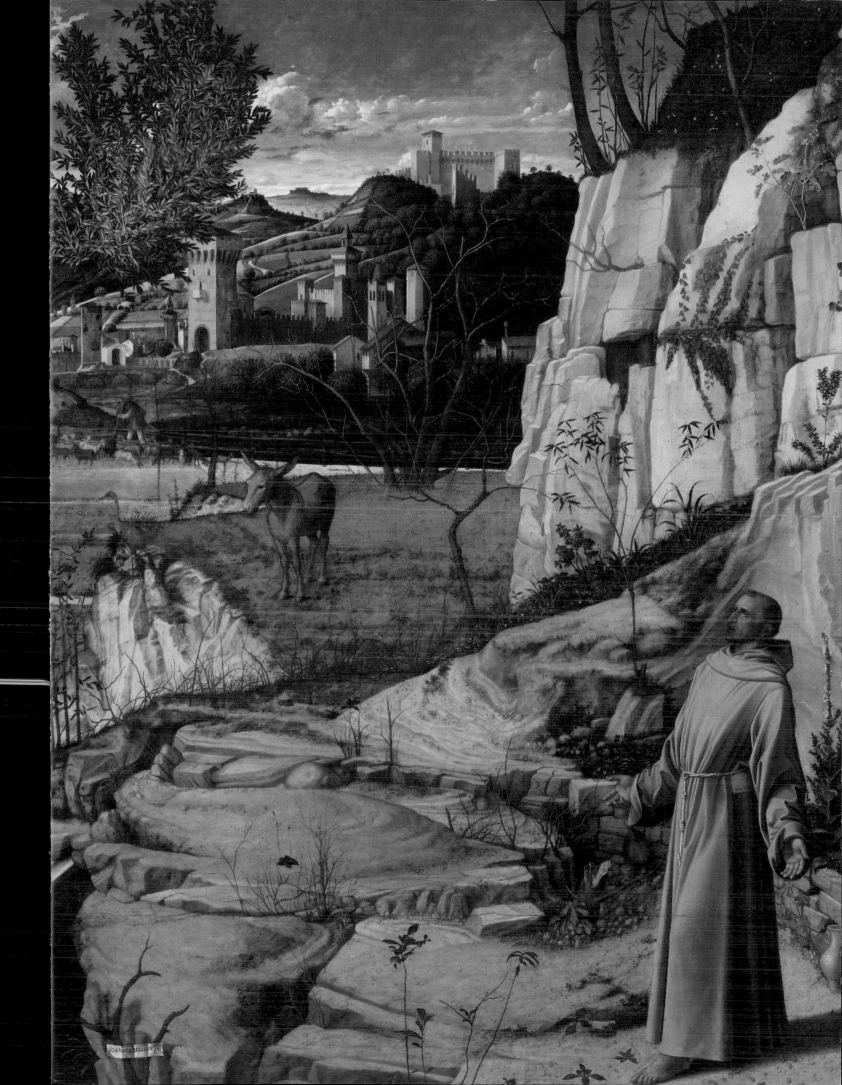